Dear Friend,

We're always looking for fun gift-giving ideas, and embroidery is one of our favorites. It's even more fun when we add special touches like appliqués, a monogram or a sprinkle of buttons. Inside, you'll find a darling pillowcase dress for a little girl, an embellished tote bag for your best friend and a pair of dishtowels for your favorite cook. There are pillows, aprons, a necklace, an autographed table topper and even a farmhouse-style clothespin bag!

Surprise your daughter, sister or best friend with a pretty hand-stitched gift...sure to be loved for years to come.

Vickie & Jo Ann

LEISURE ARTS, INC.
Little Rock, Arkansas

feather your nest

Feather Your Nest

Wouldn't this cozy picture make a sweet housewarming present? The little flowers are shapes cut from wool felt, with beads sewn to their centers. The how-to's are on page 18.

Throw

Cheerful flowers and a tall initial are pretty ways to tell everyone whose warm throw this is. On page 20, there are easy instructions for making a monogram from your favorite computer font. The flower patterns are on page 21.

Patchwork Pillow

Choose your favorite fabrics or vintage-style linens to make this pieced and embroidered pillow. Button-centered daisies and dainty wildflowers dress up solid-color rectangles. They're simple to add with easy stitches. Instructions are on page 22.

Table Topper

What a terrific way to keep family & friends close! Embroider their signatures and a heartwarming phrase on two felt circles and add a fabric center. It's a table topper your family will always cherish. How-to's are on page 24.

Bird Pillow

A cheery chirping bird greets everyone who sees him. See page 28 to cut the appliqué shapes from fabric scraps or from clothing that is no longer wearable. Once you've embroidered the design, add a button for the large flower center.

Clothespin Bag

If there's someone you know who enjoys the fresh scent of line-dried laundry, this is their perfect gift. You'll enjoy how easy it is to stitch the bag, and adding the appliqués and embroidery is just plain fun! Instructions are on page 30.

clothespins

Doll Nightgown

This doll nightgown is "sew" simple to make, you may be tempted to create one for each doll that special little girl owns. Instructions for sewing and embroidery are on page 34.

Pillowcase Dress

Oh-so adorable...that's what this
darling dress is! Easily and sweetly
sewn, embroidered with a kitten
and a special little girl's name,
it's sure to become her
warm-weather favorite.
The how-to's are
on page 32.

Tote Bag & Necklace

Here are gifts for anyone who loves flowers. On page 36, you'll find instructions for embellishing a purchased cloth tote bag with a blooming vine. The buttons are tiny baby clothes buttons! The dainty necklace is made using a covered button kit. As you can see on page 35, the bit of embroidery is quick to stitch. Choose a heartfelt charm that will have special meaning for the lucky recipient.

Pillowcase for a Girl

From the appliquéd chick to the Chicken Scratch
embroidered border, this pillowcase will look
farm-fresh on her bed. Instructions are on page 38.

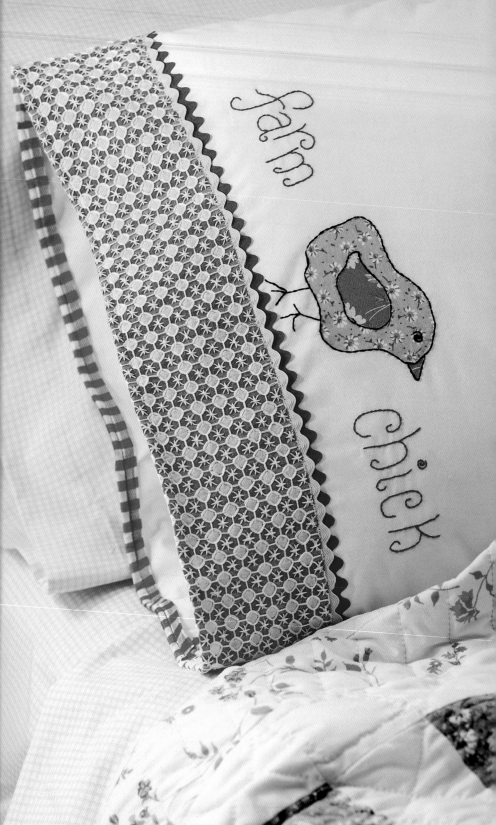

farm

chick

Pillowcase for a Boy

He's always on the move, so celebrate with a pillowcase embellished with his favorite activities. It's the stuff young dreams are made of! How-to's are on page 40.

Apron

Just because aprons are practical, it doesn't mean they can't be pretty! Instructions to sew, appliqué and embroider the handy accessory are on page 42.

Appliquéd Dishtowels

These dishtowels with happy fruit appliqués and rickrack trim may remind you of Grandma's kitchen. You're sure to know a modern cook who'd welcome their cozy, vintage style! Instructions are on page 44.

Basket Liner & Jam

By adding felt shapes and a touch of embroidery, you can repurpose an ordinary napkin as a sweet basket liner. Refresh a basket with a little paint, and you'll have a thoughtful way to present someone special with a jar of yummy Strawberry Freezer Jam.

Basket Liner & Jam

Read **Basic Instructions**,
pages 46-48

- purchased green napkin (ours has contrasting hem)
- red and green felt scraps
- 7¹/₂" square of red fabric
- green dot ribbon
- red, green and ivory embroidery floss
- natural color basket
- ivory acrylic paint
- sandpaper
- pint canning jar with lid and ring
- tissue paper

Trace strawberry and stem onto tissue paper and cut out templates. Using templates, cut strawberry from red felt and stem from green felt. Transfer embroidery patterns to felt shapes and pin shapes in place. Sewing through all layers, embroider design using 2 strands of floss. Work Chain Stitches along hemline or ¹/₂" from edge on napkin using 6 strands of floss.

Paint basket with ivory paint that has been thinned slightly with water. Dab brush onto a paper towel to remove excess moisture. Allow to dry, then sand lightly. Place napkin in basket.

For jar cover, cut a 7¹/₂" square of red fabric. Center cover over lid and tie ribbon around jar.

KEY

/   Backstitch

•   French Knot

⌐   Blanket Stitch

Strawberry Freezer Jam

Freezer jams are a snap to make and taste amazing!

4 c. sugar
2 c. strawberries, hulled and crushed
1³/₄-oz. pkg. powdered pectin
³/₄ c. water

Combine sugar and strawberries in a large mixing bowl; set aside. Whisk pectin and water together in a small saucepan; bring to a boil. Boil and stir for one minute; remove from heat. Pour pectin mixture over fruit mixture; stir until sugar dissolves, about 3 minutes. Spoon into jars leaving ¹/₂-inch headspace; secure lids. Allow to stand at room temperature for 24 hours. Store jars in freezer up to one year and opened jars in refrigerator for one month. Makes about 5 cups.

Connie Bryant
Topeka, KS

Feather Your Nest

Finished Size: 14"x14"

Read **Basic Instructions**, pages 46-48.

- 16½"x16½" piece of brown cotton fabric
- scrap of ecru wool felt
- ecru embroidery floss
- brown seed beads
- dark brown wood frame with a 14"x14" opening
- light green and medium green acrylic paints
- tissue paper
- sandpaper
- masking tape

Enlarge pattern by 125%. Transfer pattern (excluding blossoms) and embroider design using 2 strands of floss.

Trace blossoms onto tissue paper and cut out templates. Using templates, cut out blossoms from wool felt. Attach blossoms to brown fabric by sewing seed beads in centers of blossoms, stitching through all layers.

To "age" frame, lightly sand wood. Apply a "wash" (paint slightly thinned with water) of light green and allow to dry. Add a wash of medium green. Once paint has dried, sand until wood is exposed as desired.

Centering design, stretch embroidered fabric over cardboard in frame. (If frame does not have cardboard, cut a square of cardboard 14"x14".) Use masking tape to adhere edges of fabric to back of cardboard and insert cardboard into frame.

feather
your nest

KEY

Running Stitch (varying stitch length)   Straight Stitch   o   Bead placement

Stem Stitch   •   French Knot

Throw

Read **Basic Instructions**, pages 46-48.

• purchased cream solid throw (or
  2 yds of 58"w cream solid wool or
  fleece fabric)
• embroidery floss
• red 100% cotton medium weight yarn

If using yardage, trim selvages. Hem all four sides of fabric by pressing edges to wrong side ½" (twice for wool and once for fleece) and topstitching with matching thread.

Photocopy or print desired letter from your favorite font, enlarged to approximately 6"h. Transfer letter and flowers to throw. Using Stem Stitches and Satin Stitches, embroider letter with cotton yarn and flowers with 6 strands of floss. Work Blanket Stitches around edge of throw using cotton yarn.

KEY

Chain Stitch

Stem Stitch

Straight Stitch

Lazy Daisy

French Knot

Satin Stitch

Patchwork Pillow

Finished Size: 18"x18"

Read **Basic Instructions**, pages 46-48. Use $\frac{1}{4}$" seam allowances throughout.

- $\frac{1}{2}$ yd **total** of assorted print and solid fabrics for pillow top
- $18\frac{1}{2}$"x$18\frac{1}{2}$" square of print fabric for pillow back
- embroidery floss
- assorted buttons
- 18"x18" pillow form

Refer to Cutting Diagram to cut pieces from assorted fabrics for pillow top. (Diagram shows CUT sizes, not FINISHED sizes.) Sew pieces together to make pillow top. Transfer embroidery patterns to solid fabric areas of pillow top. Embroider using 3 strands of floss for large flower and French Knots and 2 strands for all other stitches. Use floss to sew buttons to centers of flowers.

Follow *Making a Knife-Edged Pillow* to complete pillow.

Cutting Diagram

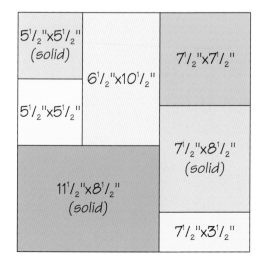

KEY

Chain Stitch (varying colors)

Stem Stitch (varying colors)

French Knot

✕   Button placement

Table Topper

Finished Size: 33" dia.

Read **Basic Instructions**, pages 46-48. Patterns are on pages 25-27.

- 36"x36" piece of blue felt
- 26"x26" piece of green felt
- 8"x8" piece of cotton floral fabric
- 8"x8" piece of paper-backed fusible web
- embroidery floss
- clear monofilament thread (optional)
- black fine ballpoint pen
- fabric glue (optional)

Referring to Fig. 1, cut a 33" dia. circle from blue felt and a 23" dia. circle from green felt with pinking shears. With 2 large "dots" opposite each other and "friends and family gather here" between dots on both sides, transfer patterns to blue felt and embroider using 6 strands of floss.

Appliqué a 7½" dia. circle of floral fabric to center of green felt. Using 3 strands of floss, Stem Stitch around appliquéd circle.

Ask friends and family members to sign their names on the green felt with ballpoint pen. Using 3 strands of floss, embroider names with Stem Stitches for letters and a French Knot to dot each "i" and "j."

Attach green felt circle to center of blue felt circle using fabric glue or layer circles without attaching so that more names can be added at a later date.

Fig. 1

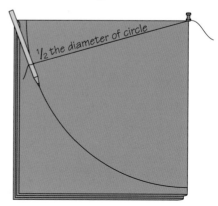

½ the diameter of circle

KEY

Stem Stitch

• French Knot

Satin Stitch

25

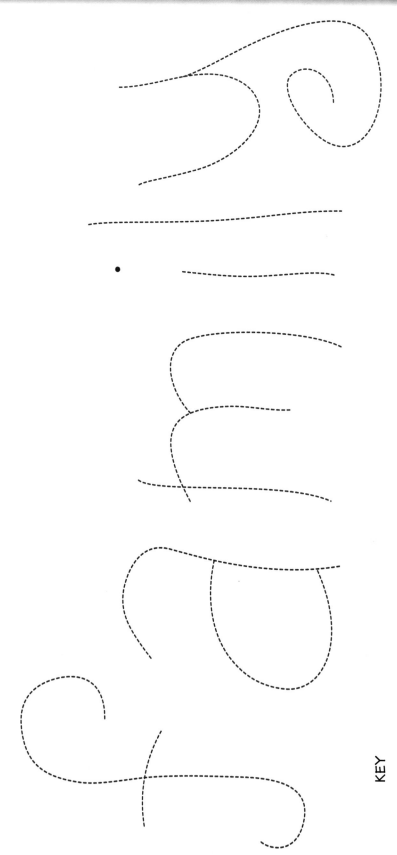

KEY

／ Stem Stitch

• French Knot

Bird Pillow

Finished Size: 16"x12"

Read **Basic Instructions**, pages 46-48.

- $^1/_2$ yd linen fabric (cut pillow top 18"x14" and pillow back 17"x13")
- $^1/_4$ yd cotton print fabric (cut 2 strips 2$^1/_2$"x40" for welting)
- cotton print scraps
- embroidery floss
- paper-backed fusible web
- 1$^3/_4$ yds $^1/_2$" dia. cord
- 12"x16" pillow form
- tissue paper
- clear monofilament thread (optional)
- water-soluble fabric pen

Enlarge pattern by 120%. Use water-soluble pen to transfer embroidery pattern to pillow top. Appliqué bird, leaf and flowers. Transfer embroidery details from pattern to appliqué pieces. Embroider using 2 strands of floss for veins in leaves and 3 strands for all other stitches and for sewing on button. Making sure design is centered, trim pillow top to 17"x13".

Use $^1/_2$" seam allowances and follow *Pillow Finishing* to make pillow with welting.

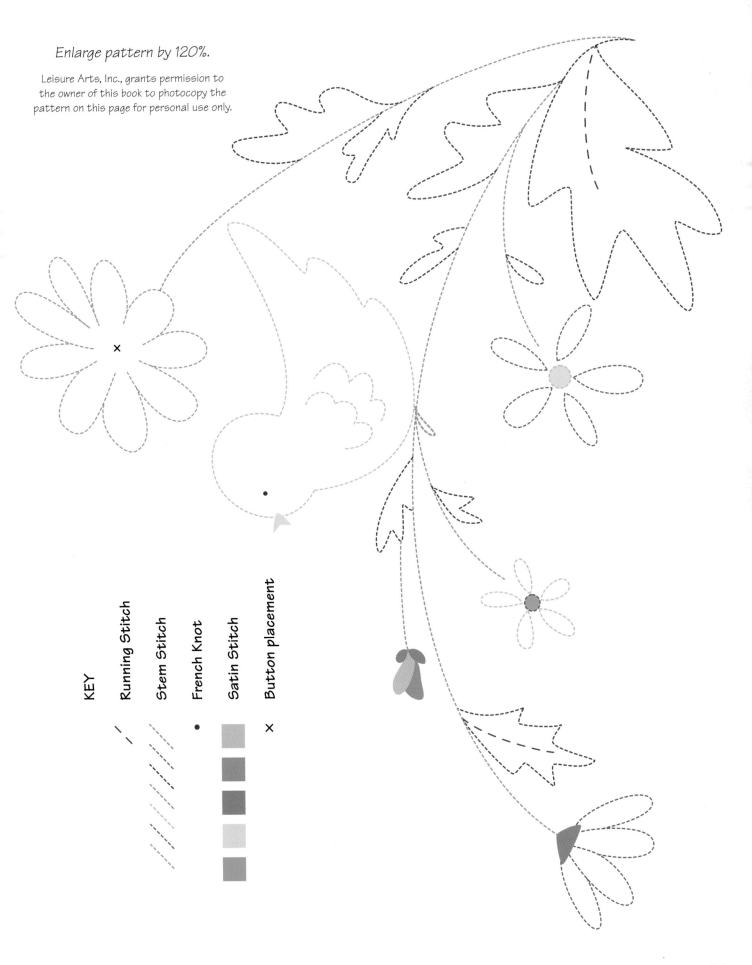

Enlarge pattern by 120%.

KEY

Running Stitch

Stem Stitch

French Knot

Satin Stitch

Button placement

Clothespin Bag

Finished Size: 13"x11½"

Read **Basic Instructions**, pages 46-48.

- 15"x27" rectangle of polka dot fabric
- 15"x27" rectangle of medium-weight fusible interfacing
- embroidery floss
- tissue paper
- clear monofilament thread (optional)
- water-soluble fabric pen
- clothespins

Fuse the interfacing to the wrong side of fabric. From fabric, cut three rectangles: 13½"x12", 13½"x9¼" and 13½"x3¾". Use water-soluble pen to transfer pattern to 13½"x9¼" rectangle. Appliqué "drying clothes." Embroider using 1 strand of floss for clothesline and bee trail, 3 strands for the word "clothespins" and 2 strands for all other stitches.

Hem one long edge of each of the two smaller rectangles, turning ¼" to wrong side twice. With right sides together and butting hemmed edges, pin smaller rectangles to large rectangle. Using ¼" seam allowances, sew small rectangles (front of bag) to large rectangle (back of bag). Clip corners and turn bag right side out. Using 3 strands of floss, Blanket Stitch along each hemmed edge.

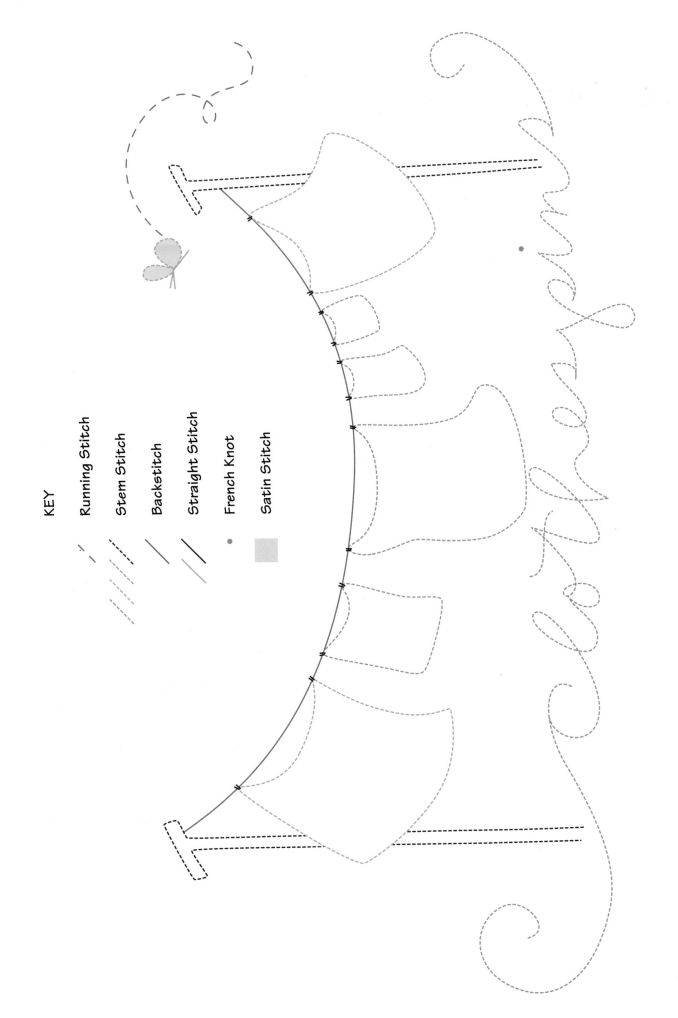

KEY

Running Stitch

Stem Stitch

Backstitch

Straight Stitch

French Knot •

Satin Stitch

Pillowcase Dress

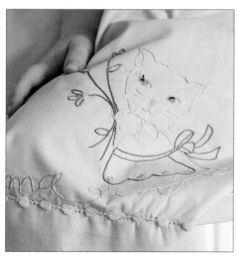

Read **Basic Instructions**, pages 46-48.

- 1 standard size pillowcase
- embroidery floss
- 2 yds of $^5/_8$"w ribbon, cut into two equal lengths
- 1$^1/_3$ yds of narrow ribbon trim
- clear monofilament thread

To make pattern for child's name, print name from computer, freehand name, or allow child to write name. (Ours is approximately 1$^1/_2$" high.) Transfer patterns to pillowcase above hemline and embroider using 2 strands of floss. Aligning trim along hemline, zigzag trim to pillowcase using clear monofilament thread in machine needle and general all-purpose thread in bobbin.

Open the closed end of the pillowcase with a seam ripper. Fold pillowcase in half lengthwise. Measure from the top of the child's shoulder to the armpit and add 1$^1/_2$". Slightly curving at sides of pillowcase, cut corners for arms the determined measurement deep and 2" wide (Fig. 1). Hem angled cuts, turning to wrong side $^1/_4$" twice. Press top raw edges $^1/_4$" and then 1" to wrong side for ribbon casings. Topstitch along bottom folded edge of each casing.

Attach a large safety pin at end of ribbon and thread one ribbon through each casing. Tie ribbon ends into bows at either side of neck.

Fig. 1

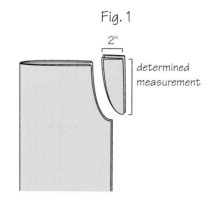

2"

determined measurement

KEY

╱   Straight Stitch

╱╱╱╱   Stem Stitch

⬭   Lazy Daisy

•   French Knot

▢▢▢   Satin Stitch

Doll Nightgown

Finished Size: 7"x9"

Read **Basic Instructions**, pages 46-48.

- $^1/_4$ yd of off-white solid fabric (cut 2 rectangles 7$^1/_2$"x10$^1/_2$" for gown front and back)
- embroidery floss
- 1$^1/_8$ yds of $^3/_8$"w ribbon, cut into two equal lengths
- $^1/_2$ yd of $^1/_2$"w purchased crocheted trim

Transfer pattern to gown front 1$^1/_2$" from bottom edge and centered horizontally. Embroider using 3 strands of floss for flowers and 1 strand for Running Stitch.

With right sides together and using $^1/_4$" seam allowances, sew long edges of gown front and back together. Cut each top corner at an angle for arms beginning on top edge 2$^1/_8$" from side seam and ending on side 3" from top edge. Hem angled cuts and bottom of gown, turning to wrong side $^1/_4$" twice. Press top raw edges $^1/_4$" and then $^3/_4$" to wrong side for ribbon casings. Topstitch along bottom folded edge of each casing.

Sew crocheted trim along bottom of gown. Using 2 strands of floss, work running stitch approximately $^1/_8$" above trim. Attach a safety pin at end of ribbon and thread one ribbon through each casing. Tie ribbon ends into bows at either side of neck.

KEY

/ Running Stitch

// Straight Stitch

⟨ Lazy Daisy

Read **Basic Instructions**, *pages 46-48*

- 1¹/₂" dia. button to cover
- polka dot fabric scrap
- felt scrap
- medium rickrack
- embroidery floss
- 1 yd of ¹/₄"w satin ribbon
- screw-type jewelry clasp
- ¹/₂" dia. button
- charm

Use backplate of button for pattern to cut circle from felt and set circle aside.

Transfer pattern onto fabric scrap and embroider design using 3 strands of floss. Follow manufacturer's instructions to cover the button, making sure stitched design is centered on button. Thread ribbon through shank of button and cut to desired length for necklace. Tie ends of ribbons to loops in clasp. Glue felt and then rickrack to back of button. Use 6 strands of floss to tie ¹/₂" dia. button and charm to ribbon.

KEY

/   **Running Stitch**

/ / / /   **Stem Stitch**

     Satin Stitch

Tote Bag

Read **Basic Instructions**, pages 46-48.

- purchased cloth tote bag
- ¼ yd coordinating fabric
- embroidery floss
- baby buttons for berries (we used 21)
- tissue paper
- water-soluble fabric pen

Measure the width of the tote bag front. Use water-soluble pen to mark band area on fabric the determined width x 4½". Beginning at center of marked area, transfer pattern to fabric. Reversing every other flower design, repeat pattern across marked area. Embroider using 6 strands for French Knots and 3 strands for remaining stitches and for sewing on buttons.

Adding ¼" to all four sides of drawn area, cut band out. Press each edge of band ¼" to wrong side. Topstitch band to tote bag front. Work Chain Stitches along top and bottom edges of band using 3 strands of floss.

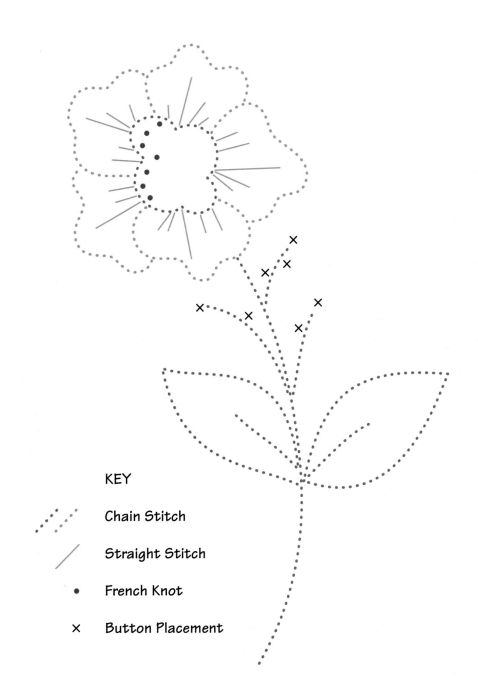

KEY

Chain Stitch

Straight Stitch

French Knot

Button Placement

Pillowcase for a Girl

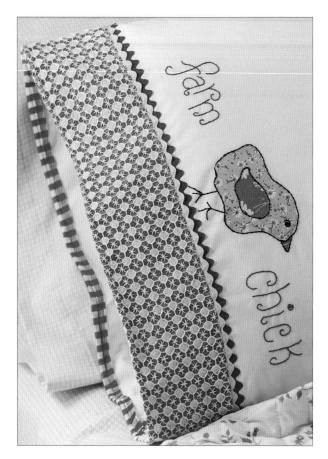

Read **Basic Instructions**, pages 46-48

- 1 white standard size pillowcase
- 1/4 yd of red and white 1/4" gingham check fabric
- scraps of cotton fabric
- embroidery floss
- 1¹/₃ yds **each** of red and yellow medium rickrack
- tissue paper
- clear monofilament thread (optional)
- water-soluble fabric pen

Use water-soluble pen to transfer pattern to pillowcase 4" from pillowcase opening. Appliqué chick body, wing and beak. Transfer chick's eye. Embroider using 3 strands of floss.

Folding under ends, topstitch red rickrack to pillowcase with center of rickrack 3¹/₂" from pillowcase opening. In the same manner, topstitch yellow rickrack with center of rickrack 3¹/₄" from pillowcase opening.

Measure the width (short end) of the pillowcase and multiply by 2. Using water soluble pen, mark area for Chicken Scratch in center of gingham check fabric 4" wide x the determined measurement. Use 3 strands of floss and follow *Chicken Scratch* instructions to embroider marked area.

For band, trim gingham to 1/4" beyond stitching on both short ends and on one long side of band (for inner edge). Trim remaining long edge (for outer edge) ³/₄" beyond stitching. Matching right sides and short edges and using a 1/4" seam allowance, sew band into a tube. Press seam allowance open. Press inner and outer edges of band 1/4" to wrong side and turn band right side out.

Slide pillowcase into band and align edge of band with center of yellow rickrack; pin band in place and topstitch along inner edge. Fold outer edge of band to inside of pillowcase and topstitch in place.

farm

KEY

Backstitch

French Knot

chick

Pillowcase for a Boy

Read **Basic Instructions**, pages 46-48.

• 1 standard size pillowcase
• embroidery floss
• 1 1/3 yds of jumbo rickrack
• 1 1/3 yds of narrow ribbon trim
• clear monofilament thread
• water-soluble fabric pen

Using water-soluble pen and ruler, mark desired placement of rickrack on pillowcase (at least 2" from opening). Transfer patterns to pillowcase top as desired, leaving 1/2" space on each side of drawn line. Embroider using 3 strands of floss. Scatter additional French Knots as desired.

Centering on drawn line and turning under ends, sew rickrack and ribbon trim around pillowcase using a zigzag stitch and clear monofilament thread in machine needle and general all-purpose thread in bobbin.

jump

ride

skip

run

climb

tiptoe

KEY

/ /   Backstitch

• •   French Knot

▨   Satin Stitch

Apron

Finished Length: 18½" long

Read **Basic Instructions**, pages 46-48.

- 1⅝ yds of heavy cotton fabric (cut 36½"x15" piece for the apron skirt, 4½"x36" piece for the bottom trim and 5½"x90" strip [pieced as needed] for the waistband)
- cotton fabric scraps
- brown embroidery floss
- 2 – ⅞" dia. buttons
- 13 – ⁷⁄₁₆" dia. buttons
- paper-backed fusible web
- tissue paper
- clear monofilament thread (optional)
- water-soluble fabric pen

Press side edges of apron skirt ¼" to wrong side; press ¼" to wrong side again. Press all edges of bottom trim ¼" to wrong side, then press trim in half lengthwise. Aligning side edges and overlapping skirt with trim by ½", insert bottom edge of skirt between long edges of trim and pin in place. Topstitch approximately ⅛" from top edge of trim, stitching through all layers. Topstitch sides of skirt and trim, stitching through all layers.

Use water-soluble pen to transfer utensils, mitt and trim patterns to apron, repeating pattern for trim. Appliqué utensils and mitt. Transfer embroidery details onto appliqués. Embroider and sew on buttons using 2 strands of floss.

Referring to Fig. 1, pin two box pleats along top edge of skirt. Baste pleats in place.

Press all edges of waistband ¼" to wrong side and then press waistband in half lengthwise. Centering waistband and overlapping skirt with waistband by ½", insert top edge of skirt between long edges of waistband and pin in place. Topstitch sides and bottom edge of entire waistband approximately ⅛" from edges, catching skirt in stitching.

Transfer flower patterns to top of apron and embroider and sew on buttons using 2 strands of floss.

Fig. 1

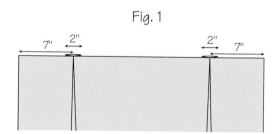

KEY

/ Stem Stitch

• French Knot

✗ Button placement

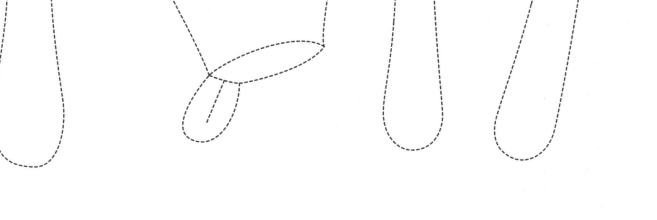

Appliquéd Dishtowels

Read **Basic Instructions**, pages 46-48.

• 2 green and white dishtowels
• orange solid and red mini check fabric scraps
• red and orange jumbo rickrack (To determine length of each color of rickrack needed, measure width of dishtowel and add 1".)
• red embroidery floss
• paper-backed fusible web
• tissue paper
• clear monofilament thread (optional)
• water-soluble fabric pen

    Appliqué orange and apple (including arms and legs) to dishtowels. Use water-soluble pen to transfer embroidery details. Embroider using 3 strands of floss for Stem Stitches and French Knots and 2 strands for Running Stitches and Straight Stitches.

    Folding ends to the back of towel, topstitch rickrack across width of each towel.

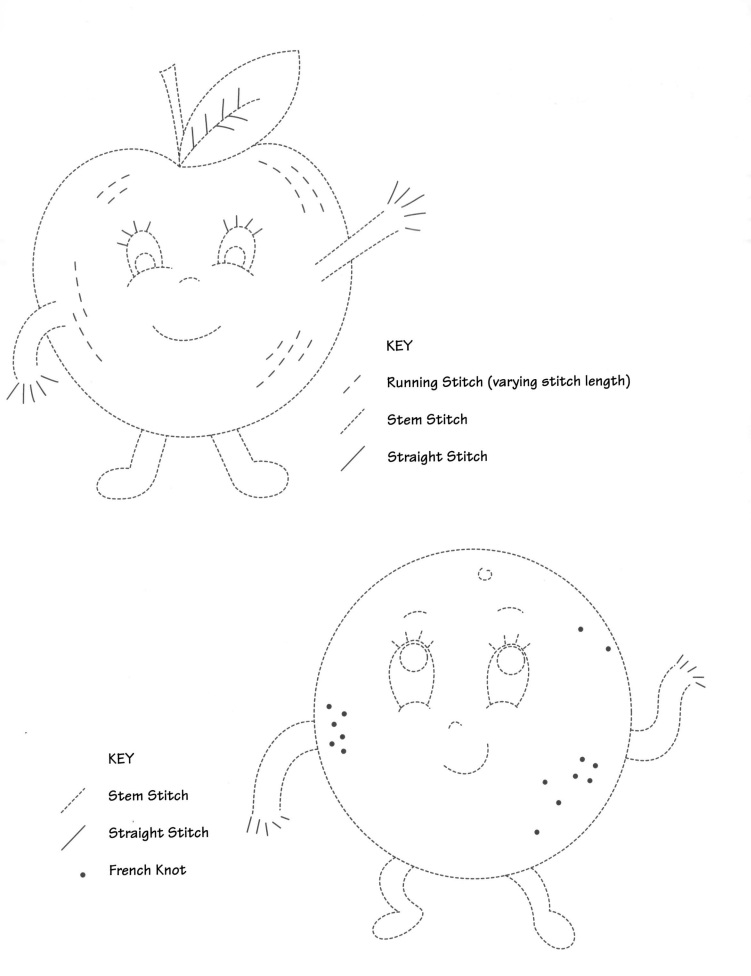

KEY

Running Stitch (varying stitch length)

Stem Stitch

Straight Stitch

KEY

Stem Stitch

Straight Stitch

French Knot

45

Basic Instructions

Embroidery Stitches

Use 3 strands of embroidery floss for all stitches unless otherwise indicated in project instructions. Follow the stitch diagrams to bring the needle up at odd numbers and down at even numbers.

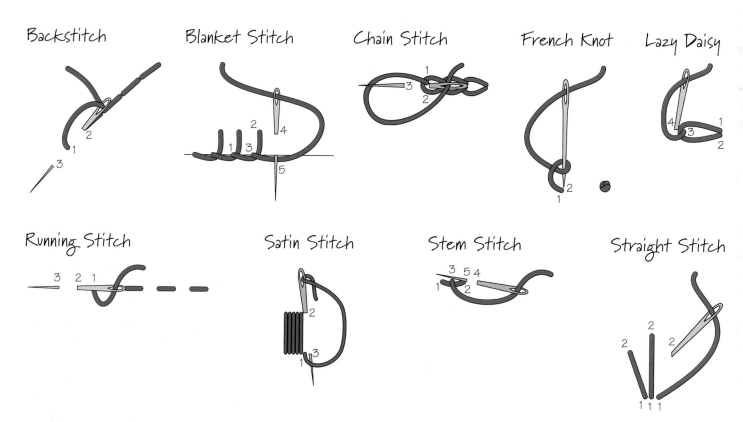

Backstitch   Blanket Stitch   Chain Stitch   French Knot   Lazy Daisy

Running Stitch   Satin Stitch   Stem Stitch   Straight Stitch

Chicken Scratch

For the Chicken Scratch design on page 38, complete all of the stitches in a small area before moving to the next area. Begin the design by working a Smryna Cross in each dark red square (Fig. 1). Next, work a Straight Stitch across the center of each light red square (Fig. 2). To make the diamond on each white square, bring the needle up and thread it under the Straight Stitches twice before taking it down (Fig. 3).

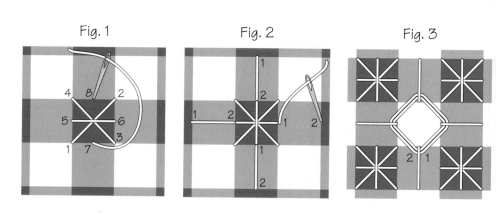

Fig. 1   Fig. 2   Fig. 3

Pre-washing

We recommend that cotton and linen fabrics be washed, dried and pressed before cutting. Also, purchased items, such as towels and pillowcases that will be used and laundered later, should be washed and dried before making projects. Do not use fabric softener.

Fabric Appliqué

Several of our projects include fabric appliqués for added charm and interest. For your appliqués, choose medium weight 100% cotton fabrics.

For appliqué pieces, you will need to reverse the patterns. To make a reversed pattern, trace appliqué shape onto tissue paper, turn tissue paper over and re-trace the drawn lines. Trace this reversed pattern onto the paper-side of fusible web.

Rough cut pieces from web approximately 1/4" outside drawn lines. Follow manufacturer's instructions to fuse web pieces to wrong side of fabrics. Cut pieces out along outer drawn lines. Remove paper backing and fuse to background, following transferred lines for placement.

To make your appliqués more durable, you may choose to zigzag all raw edges of the appliqués using clear monofilament thread in the machine needle and general all-purpose thread in the bobbin.

Transferring Patterns

There are many ways to transfer a pattern onto fabric. Pick the method that works best with the fabric and project you've chosen. If adding fused appliqués to your project, use the *Water-Soluble Fabric Pen* method since other methods may smear or set when fabric is pressed.

The instructions for the Tote Bag on page 36 call for the pattern to be reversed. To reverse the pattern, trace pattern onto tissue paper, turn tissue paper over and re-trace drawn lines.

Water-Soluble Fabric Pen
- water-soluble fabric pen
- tissue paper (optional)

If the fabric is sheer enough, place the pattern under the fabric and trace the pattern with water-soluble pen. If you can't quite see through the fabric, trace the pattern onto tissue paper and tape it and the fabric to a sunny window; then, trace the pattern onto the fabric. Embroider the design.

Note: If adding fusible appliqués, the steam from the iron may remove some of the drawn lines; re-apply as needed.

Tissue Paper
- tissue paper

Trace the pattern onto tissue paper and pin it to the fabric. Embroider the design, stitching through the tissue paper. When you're finished, carefully tear away the tissue paper.

Iron-on Transfer Pen or Pencil
- tissue paper
- permanent iron-on transfer pen or pencil

Trace the pattern onto tissue paper. Turn the paper over and use transfer pen to draw over the lines on the back of the paper. Place the inked side on the fabric. Use a dry iron at a low setting and press one area for a few seconds; then, lift the iron and move to another area until the whole design is transferred. (Do not iron back and forth which might smear the lines.) Embroider the design, covering the transferred lines with the stitching.

Transfer Paper
- tissue paper (optional)
- wax-free transfer paper
- ball point pen

If you wish, first trace the pattern onto tissue paper. Place the transfer paper, colored side down, between the fabric and the pattern. Use ball point pen to draw over the design. Embroider the design.

Pillow Finishing

Adding Welting to a Pillow Top

Sew the strips for welting called for in project together, end to end, to make one continuous strip.

Lay cord along center of strip on wrong side of fabric; fold strip over cord. Using a zipper foot, machine baste along length of strip close to cord. Trim seam allowance to ½".

Matching raw edges and beginning and ending 3" from ends of welting, baste welting to right side of pillow top. To make turning corners easier, clip seam allowance of welting at pillow top corners.

Remove approximately 3" of seam at 1 end of welting; fold fabric away from cord. Trim remaining end of cord so that cord ends meet exactly.

Fold remaining short edge of welting fabric ½" to wrong side; fold fabric back over area where ends meet (Fig. 4). Baste remainder of welting to pillow top close to cord.

Fig. 4

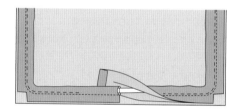

Follow Making a Knife-Edge Pillow to complete pillow.

Making a Knife-Edge Pillow

Place pillow back and pillow top right sides together. Using seam allowance called for in project and leaving an opening for turning, sew pillow top and back together.

Turn pillow right side out, carefully pushing corners outward. Stuff with polyester fiberfill or pillow form and sew final closure by hand.

Credits

Designers: Becky Werle, Kim Hamblin, Anne Pulliam Stocks, and Lori Wenger
Editorial Writer: Susan McManus Johnson
Technical Editor: Lisa Lancaster
Technical Writer: Frances Huddleston
Graphic Artist: Amy Temple
Production Artist: Janie Wright
Photo Stylist: Christy Myers
Photographer: Mark Matthews

We want to extend a warm thank you to The DMC Corporation for the embroidery floss.